Bridges Connect

Bridges Connect

a building block book

Lee Sullivan Hill

Carolrhoda Books, Inc./Minneapolis

For the students at Salisbury Central School and for Mrs. Dowd and Mrs. Mayland, all of whom helped me build bridges.—L. S. H.

For metric conversion, when you know the number of miles, multiply by 1.61 to find the number of kilometers. When you know the number of feet, multiply by 30.48 to find the number of centimeters.

The photographs in this book are reproduced through the courtesy of: Jo-Ann Ordano, front cover, p. 15; Don Eastman, back cover, pp. 2, 7, 12, 25; Howard Ande, pp. 1, 21, 22, 27; Jerry Hennen, pp. 5, 13, 16, 23; Bob Firth, pp. 6, 17; British Tourist Authority, p. 8; Betty Crowell, p. 9; Tony LaGruth, pp. 10–11, 14; Kim Karpeles, pp. 18, 28; Douglas Steakley, pp. 19, 20, 29; D. J. Lambrecht, p. 24; Cheryl Koenig Morgan, p. 26.

Carolrhoda Books, Inc. c/o The Lerner Group
241 First Avenue North, Minneapolis, MN 55401

Library of Congress Cataloging-in-Publication Data

Hill, Lee Sullivan, 1958–
   Bridges connect / by Lee Sullivan Hill.
     p.   cm. — (A Building block book)
   Summary: Introduces different kinds of bridges, their materials, construction, and maintenance.
   ISBN 1-57505-021-8
   1. Bridges—Juvenile literature. [1.Bridges] I. Title. II. Series.
TG148.H35 1996
624′.2—dc20
                                      96–5406

Manufactured in the United States of America
1 2 3 4 5 6 SP 02 01 00 99 98 97

Bridges. They hang in space as if by magic.
Bridges carry us over water, or train tracks,
or busy roads. They connect one land to another.

Bridges can be small. A log over water is
really a bridge.

Bridges can be big. The Coos Bay Bridge is
more than a mile long. It goes low, then up high,
then low again.

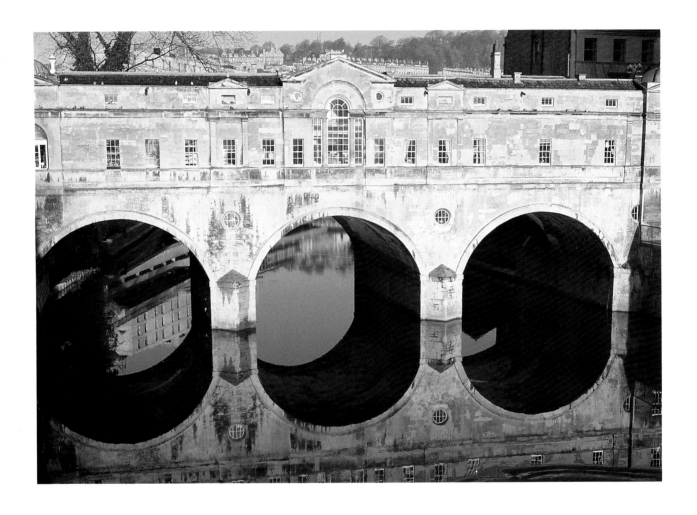

A building can even be a bridge. From a
window on the Pulteney Bridge in England, you
can watch the water flow below.

Some bridges are new. Where roads meet, people in cars wait and wait at red lights. Building new bridges can solve the problem. Some cars go under bridges. Other cars go over the top. No one waits at red lights anymore.

Some bridges are old.
Years ago, bridge builders
used wood. But wet
wood can rot. The bridge
could fall apart. Builders
added walls and a roof to
keep off rain and snow.
They wanted covered
bridges to last.

The West Cornwall Bridge still crosses the
Housatonic River. It has lasted more than one
hundred years.

The outside is painted red like a barn. The inside is dark like a tunnel. Car tires go "Bump, bump!" over the wooden floor.

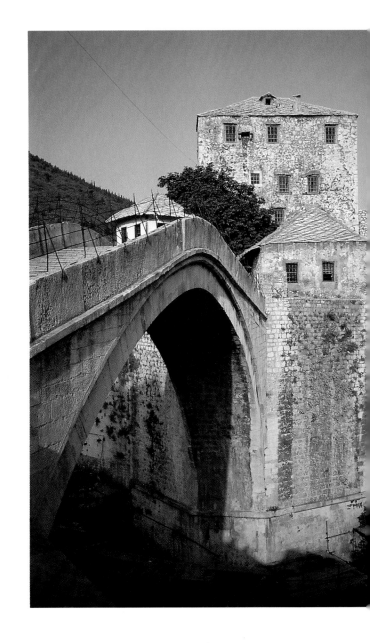

When builders wanted stronger bridges, they used stone instead of wood. (One of the Three Little Pigs did the same thing to make his house sturdy.)

An arch can make a stone bridge even
stronger. Stone arches have a keystone in the
middle. If you pulled it out, the bridge would
fall down.

For some bridges, builders used iron. Iron chains hung down from tall towers. The chains held the bridge deck, or floor, way up in the air.

But iron can be brittle. Engineers began to use steel cables in place of iron chains. These steel bridges are called suspension bridges.

Tall ships sail under the Brooklyn Bridge. Just look at the web of cables!

Suspension bridges stand tall, but drawbridges move. Watch a drawbridge lift its deck. The whole road goes in the air. Boats pass through. Then the deck comes back down. Cars can cross the drawbridge again.

Cars can't drive across all bridges. Only people use skywalks. Inside a skywalk, you'll stay warm and dry. You'll also have a great view of the cars below.

People make sure that all bridges are safe and strong. Workers replace old beams with new ones. They fix holes in the deck. Painters paint steel so it won't rust.

A story is told about painters on the Golden
Gate Bridge. That bridge is *so* long, by the time
the painters paint from one end to the other,
it's time to start all over again!

Bridges like the Golden Gate make you open your eyes wide. They are so grand.

The Bear Mountain Bridge makes you close
your eyes. It is skinny and scary and very, very
high. The edge is right there, next to your car
window. Don't look down!

Open your eyes. Look up at a bridge over train tracks. The straight tracks run on and on. A faraway light comes closer and closer. A train ROARS toward you. Then it's gone. Left behind, the same straight tracks run on and on, under the bridge and beyond.

Look down from the top of a wooden bridge.
Are there cracks between the boards? When you
cross over, pretend to be one of the Billy Goats
Gruff. Hurry! You might run into a troll.

Look up from under
a bridge and see how it is
made. See how rectangles
and triangles fit together.
Imagine how the bridge
stays up there, in the air.

You can build a bridge out of blocks, or sticks, or books. When you grow up, you could build a bridge out of steel.

You could become an engineer and plan
bridges. You could work for a construction
company and build bridges. Or you could even
be a painter and paint bridges from one end to
the other, forever and ever.

Bridges connect in many ways. They bring
people together. They carry cars and trucks and
trains over anything in their way. They connect
one place to another.

Bridges are almost like magic.

A Photo Index to the Bridges in This Book

 **Cover** The San Francisco-Oakland Bay Bridge connects Oakland and San Francisco, California. It is really like two bridges put together. The bay bridge crosses from one city to an island in the middle of the bay, then over to the other city. There is a tunnel on Yerba Buena Island, in between the two bridge parts. The San Francisco-Oakland Bay Bridge opened in 1936, just six months before the Golden Gate Bridge.

 **Page 1** This wooden bridge is in Litchfield, Connecticut. It curves gently over a stream beside a pond. You could make a lot of noise running across its wooden floorboards.

 **Page 2** The Tower Bridge in London, England, was built in 1894. Its towers look like castles floating on the Thames River.

 **Page 5** The Royal Gorge suspension bridge in Colorado doesn't really hang from space, but it seems to. It hangs from steel cables held up by towers. There are five suspension bridges in this book. Can you find them?

 **Page 6** A log across a brook acts as a beam bridge. A beam bridge is simple, but it can help you understand the parts of any bridge. In this beam bridge, the banks of the brook are its supports, or *abutments*. The distance between bridge supports is called the *span*. Some bridges have supports, called *piers*, in the middle. This bridge, however, needs none. The floor of a bridge is known as the *deck*. In this case, the top of the log is the bridge deck.

 **Page 7** Coos Bay Bridge is 1 mile and 25 feet long, to be exact. It is dedicated to the engineer who planned it: Conde B. McCullough.

 **Page 8** There are shops on the Pulteney Bridge in Bath, England. It was built over 200 years ago.

 **Page 9** The Newhall Pass has more than one bridge, or overpass. Highways 14 and 5 in California criss-cross here on the northern edge of the San Fernando Valley.

 **Pages 10 and 11** The West Cornwall Bridge was built in 1864. There were many trees in northwestern Connecticut at that time. So builders used wood trusses for the structure. Trusses, made of many pieces of wood connected together, can reach farther than simple boards.

 **Page 12** This bridge over the Neretva River was built in 1566. It lasted for over 400 years until a bomb destroyed it in 1993 during the war in Bosnia.

 Page 13 You can ride on a bike path right over this stone arch bridge. It was built in Wisconsin in 1881. Gravity pulls the sides of the arch toward each other. They lean on each other and do not fall down. The center block of stone where the two sides meet is the keystone.

 **Pages 14 and 15** In 1883, a huge steel suspension bridge opened after years of planning. The famous Brooklyn Bridge over New York Harbor spans 1,595 feet. At the time it was built, it was the longest bridge in the world. Washington Roebling and Emily Warren Roebling worked together to design and build the bridge.

 **Page 16** This photograph was taken from a boat on the Illinois River. You can see the sides of the drawbridge hanging open in the air. Did you notice that the Tower Bridge (on page 2) is also a movable bridge?

 Page 17 This skywalk passes right over Robert Street in Saint Paul, Minnesota. In Minnesota, skywalks are called skyways. What would you call them?

 Page 18 Ironworkers repair the Wabash Avenue Bridge in Chicago. All bridges need maintenance. Older bridges, made when cars and trucks were lighter and slower, sometimes need to be rebuilt.

 **Pages 19 and 20** The Golden Gate Bridge spans the entrance to San Francisco Bay in California. It was completed in 1937. The chief engineer, Joseph Baermann Strauss, headed a team of the best civil engineers of that time. The architect, Irving F. Morrow, chose the bridge's famous red-orange paint.

Page 21 Bear Mountain Bridge crosses the Hudson River near Peekskill, New York. The roadway seems to run right into a mountain. Driving across the Bear Mountain Bridge takes courage. There are only two lanes, one going in each direction.

Page 22 This train is passing under Route 112 in Huntington, Massachusetts. The bridge carrying the roadway was built in the 1930s. Like a highway overpass, it lets cars cross over the tracks without waiting.

Page 23 Do you know the story of the Three Billy Goats Gruff? Or did you ever read about Winnie the Pooh playing on a bridge? Bridges are great places to pretend. Under a bridge, you might find a secret place to sit. On top of a bridge, you could be crossing a moat into a castle.

Page 24 A structure holds up a bridge, the way your skeleton holds up your body. Columns run up and down. Beams run side to side. Cross braces run diagonally, or at an angle. The structure holds the bridge together. The steel "bones" in this photograph hold up Route 154 in Santa Barbara, California.

Page 25 The Astoria Bridge crosses the Columbia River in Astoria, Oregon. From far away, its structure looks like rectangles and triangles stacked together.

Page 26 Wooden blocks make good bridges. But almost anything will do. What kinds of bridges can you build?

Page 27 Painters high up on the Bear Mountain Bridge wear safety harnesses, just in case.

Page 28 These preschool children are just having fun on an old wooden footbridge. Bridges really do bring people together, in many different ways.

Page 29 The San Francisco-Oakland Bay Bridge glitters at night.